THE CAMPAIGN IN INDIA

Dedicated by Permission to

Her Most Gracious Majesty The Queen

THE CAMPAIGN IN INDIA

Captain G. F. Atkinson

Foreword Mushirul Hasan

This book is a collaborative effort between the
NATIONAL ARCHIVES OF INDIA and NIYOGI BOOKS

Published by

NIYOGI BOOKS
D-78, Okhla Industrial Area, Phase-I
New Delhi-110 020, India
Tel: 91-11-26816301, 49327000
Fax: 91-11-26810483, 26813830
email: niyogibooks@gmail.com
www.niyogibooks.com

ISBN: 978-93-81523-37-7
Year of Publication: 2012

Printed at: Niyogi Offset Pvt. Ltd., New Delhi, India

Contents

Foreword

The story of the 1857 revolt began in Meerut on 10 May 1857, and concluded with the final assault from the Ridge upon the Kashmiri Gate in September. The revolt spread all over the United Provinces and Delhi and partly in Central India and Bihar. 'Without faith in God,' said Maulvi Zakaullah, the historian living in Delhi, 'I could never have got through that period of horror and dismay. But worse was yet to follow; and it was in the last stage of all, when we were entirely homeless, that prayers helped me most of all.'

At the head of the revolt was Bahadur Shah Zafar, the Mughal emperor who bemoaned his fate in Urdu *ghaza*ls. Brave men and women, notably Lakshmi Bai, or the Rani of Jhansi, aided him. But the British generals and soldiers sealed their fate. The Queen's Proclamation of 1858, i.e., the end of Company rule and the transfer of its powers to the Crown, marked the triumph of British colonialism and India's subjugation.

In 2008, I introduced *Mutiny Memoirs* by Colonel A.R.D. Mackenzie; the reprint carries a detailed introduction. Now, I am happy to introduce another interesting story of the great upheaval. It is told by Captain Atkinson with the aid of sketches. Sadly, however, there is not much information about him in the National Archives. Perhaps, a more extensive search may yield some results.

This book illustrates the progress, rather than the process, leading to the siege of Delhi and its recapture. The principal events of the 1857 revolt are represented but only as pointers to the imminent victory of the British army. This is, therefore, a one-sided and inconclusive story. And yet, it must be accessed to understand how the imperial mind moulded attitudes of discourses.

Our mission at the National Archives of India is to reprint some of the old books in our library collection. I am happy that Niyogi Books has agreed to undertake the publication of this book and make it accessible to the readers. I invite other publishers to do the same.

Mushirul Hasan
Director-General, National Archives of India

To Her Most Gracious Majesty the Queen

MADAM,

WHEN a remorselessly treacherous and rebellious foe sought to uproot the British Power in India, and by acts of deliberately-planned ferocity and fiendish cruelty strove to destroy every European and Christian in the land, the devoted heroism of a small but resolute force, who fought to maintain the rights of their Sovereign and the honour of England, was so far crowned with success as to stay the arm of the destroyer, wrenching from his grasp the stronghold of rebellion, and winning for them not only victory in the crime-stained streets of Delhi, but the proud satisfaction of YOUR MAJESTY'S gracious approval and heart-felt sympathy.

Though opposed to all but overpowering numbers, in long-continued, close, and deadly conflict, amidst scorching heat and withering pestilence, by night and day, that band of heroes, when the fate of India vibrated in the balance, would not suffer a thought of any other result than, under the blessing of Almighty God, a victorious one, that should re-establish the sway of YOUR MAJESTY'S sceptre in the most splendid province of the Empire.

Undeterred by the protracted hardships of the siege, assault, and capture of Delhi, the glorious victors hastened to the rescue of their beleaguered countrymen and their families in Oude, gathering fresh laurels on the way, and taking share in the rescue of the suffering but heroic garrison of Lucknow.

The following Sketches, imperfect as they are, which, by permission graciously accorded, I respectfully dedicate to Your Majesty, will perhaps afford a faint idea of some of the scenes which that gallant force went through in honour of their country and for love of their Queen.

I am,

MADAM,

With the most profound respect,

Your Majesty's most faithful and devoted

Subject and Servant,

GEORGE FRANCKLIN ATKINSON,

Captain, Bengal Engineers.

THE CAMPAIGN IN INDIA: 1857-58

Capt. G. F. Atkinson, del[t] London, Day & Son, Lithographers to the Queen, Gate Shreet, Lincoln's Inn Fields. E. Walker lith.

No 1. Sepoys At Rifle Practice

1 Sepoys At Rifle Practice

THE causes which led to the Mutiny of the Bengal Army will, in all probability, remain for ever a matter of conjecture. So many conflicting opinions are entertained regarding this terrible revolt, that it is impossible to arrive at any conclusion that can satisfactorily account for a disaster which, awful and appalling in its nature, has already been productive of much good. Like a fearful tempest it fell upon the land, scattering ruin and destruction around ; but in the havoc it created, the air—impregnated with pestilential vapours—was cleared, and the long-impending storm has, we may all fervently hope, produced a calm,—not that dangerous calm which forebodes the coming gale, but a settled and abiding quiet, which may endure for ages to come.

There are many who profess to have foreseen the approaching disaster, and who attribute it entirely to the fatal acts of the Government in pampering the native soldiery by yielding to them in their every wish, and succumbing to them whenever they evinced opposition ; by withdrawing from commanding officers all power and authority over their men, until the Sepoys recognized in them nought but a cipher; —to this, above all, it is conceived that the lax state of discipline in the Bengal army arose. But to this it is objected, that the Sepoys of the Madras and Bombay armies were subjected to an identical state of things as regards the power and influence of commanding officers, and that they, as armies, did not mutiny. Others consider that the vast extension of our territory during the last few years tended more than anything else to create a feeling of dissatisfaction in the army. Men whose homes were in Oude, and who had hitherto been able to enjoy the opportunity of spending their leave with their families from whom they were never separated by any extraordinary distance, now found themselves ordered away to be quartered for years in Scinde, or the Punjab, or in Burmah, without any corresponding advantages : but this feeling of dissatisfaction might have smouldered for ever ; and though a spark of mutiny may have flashed here and there, such alone would never have ignited the whole army into a blaze of rebellion.

Then there are those who clearly recognize the cause of the Mutiny in the annexation of Oude, and maintain that the agents of the Royal family, knowing accurately the disaffected state of the native troops, found in them willing tools by which they could accomplish their own crafty ends; that they found the army conscious of its might, fully ripe for revolt, and they only bided their time until some fitting opportunity should occur. Nor had they long to wait. It is well known how tenacious is the Sepoy of his *caste*, and how suspicious he is of anything that is likely to affect his religion. The greater part—probably four-fifths—of the army being Hindoos, and more than half of these being Brahmins, known to be the most bigoted of their race, their influence was paramount; and, credulous to a degree as is the native mind, it was only for the agents of the Oude Royal family to obtain some plausible tale that it was the intention of the British Government to force them to adopt Christianity, and then the overthrow of British supremacy was a mere matter of time.

A pretext was readily afforded them by the introduction into the native army of the new Enfield rifles, the cartridges of which were made up with a mixture of cows' fat and hogs' lard, to taste which was sufficient to destroy the Sepoys' caste; and however varied may be the opinions regarding the original causes that tended to the great Mutiny, there is but one universally entertained, that the torch which created the conflagration was this matter of the greased cartridges. Whether the weapon was handled by the agents of the King of Oude, or by any other ambitious and designing native princes, may remain a conjecture; whether the state of the army was ripened to revolt by the disaffection arising from the extended frontier, or from want of power in the hands of the European officers, or from any other causes, there is no question about it, that the native army were impressed with the idea that it was the object of the Government to coerce them into the profession of Christianity, and that the new Commander-in-Chief had been sent from England expressly for the purpose of carrying it out. The sensation thus created was of no ordinary kind, and wise men clearly saw that some terrible disaster would befall if the use of the cartridges was persisted in.

This is not the place, however, for entering more fully into the events that occurred from the time when the 19th regiment broke into open mutiny on the 25th of February, when it positively refused to receive the cartridges, until the memorable 10th of May, when the storm burst at Meerut with all its violence: suffice it to say, that from January to May the matter of the greased cartridges was unquestionably the pretext for the insurrection, and that through it the credulous minds of the Sepoys were thoroughly impressed with the idea (to such an extent that no arguments of their officers could in any way dissipate it) that they were to be Christianized; and rather than submit to this, they joined heart and hand in endeavouring to overthrow the British power, and massacre every Christian in the country.

The Government, early in 1857, had established at the principal stations Schools of Musketry, where detachments from every regiment in the service were sent to become instructed in the use of the new weapon. The Vignette represents a party of Sepoys who have joined at practice, and to whom has been communicated the nature of the cartridges.

Capt. G. F. Atkinson, del[t] London, Day & Son, Lithographers to the Queen, Gate Shreet, Lincoln's Inn Fields. W. Simpson, lith.

N[o] 2. The 1st Bengal Fusiliers Marching Down From Dugshai.

2 The First Bengal Fusiliers Marching Down From Dugshai

THIS Sketch represents the March of the 1st Bengal Fusiliers from the Hill station of Dugshai for the Plains, to join the force assembling at Umballa for the purpose of retaking the city of Delhi from the hands of the mutineers.

Dugshai is one of three military stations situated on the first range of the Himalayahs, and is about 7,000 feet above the level of the sea. The other two stations are Subathoo and Kussowlie, each situated at a distance of ten miles from each other. Kussowlie being nine miles from the foot of the hills, is reached by a steep and narrow road; further on, but at a lower level, not above 4,500 feet above the sea, is situated Subathoo, on the road to Simla, which is twenty miles further north. To connect Simla with the Plains by a road accessible for wheeled vehicles, a new line was traced, which, leaving Kussowlie and Subathoo, passed near the station of Dugshai, at a distance of twenty miles from the Plains.

Subathoo for many years had been the quarters of a local battalion of Hill-men called Goorkahs (a race of men who have highly distinguished themselves wherever they have been engaged), when Lord Ellenborough, as Governor-General, observing the advantage of locating the British troops in the cool and invigorating climate of the Himalayahs, removed the Goorkah battalion to new quarters close to Simla, and caused barracks to be erected at Subathoo and Kussowlie.

Finding the benefit that followed this arrangement, a third station was a few years later selected at Dugshai, which is situated on a bare and lofty mountain, but which, though not so attractive, from want of foliage, is nevertheless the mot salubrious of the three, and from its position might with very slight fortifications be made a Gibraltar of the Himalayahs.

It was at these three stations that the British infantry, that fought so gallantly at Delhi, were quartered when the tidings came of the revolt at Meerut of the 10th May. One the 12th an aide-de-camp galloped through Kussowlie conveying the intelligence to General Anson, then at Simla: that same afternoon Her Majesty's 75th marched off from Kussowlie for Umballa, and on the following day the 1st Fusiliers received instructions to follow with the utmost expedition. In two hours the regiment was under arms, and in light marching order, without jackets, started joyfully on their mission, amidst cheers which will never be forgotten by those who heard them.

This gallant regiment, on whose colours are emblazoned the names of battles fought and won, from Plassey down to the taking of Burmah, marched gladly forth to reap that harvest of laurels which they successively gained both at Delhi and Lucknow. How they bore the brunt of many a hard-fought field, the following pages will tend to show; and the list of casualties, which by the official returns show that 319 fell or were wounded out of 427, tells its own tale.

The regiment marched that night thirty miles; and a trying time was it for men who, from a cool English climate, were suddenly brought down to encounter the fiery heat of a May day in the burning plains of India, with no protection for them but the shade of a few small trees, under which they bivouacked. The following day found them in Umballa at the end of their sixty miles march.

The 2nd Fusiliers, who were quartered at Subathoo, followed on the succeeding day; and these were the three weak British regiments of foot who, with the assistance of 400 of Her Majesty's 60th Rifles upheld the honour of Old England for so many weeks before Delhi, and who, amidst pestilence and the terrors of a withering climate, fought so desperately and so successfully against such fearful odds.

Capt. G. F. Atkinson, del[t] London, Day & Son, Lithographers to the Queen, Gate Shreet, Lincoln's Inn Fields. E. Walker lith.

No 3. Officers Joining The Force.

3 Officers Joining The Force

In consequence of the heavy loss which was experienced in officers during the continuous actions before Delhi, it was found necessary to apply to the local Government of the Punjab to spare as many officers as they could from regiments not engaged before Delhi; and gladly was the opportunity taken advantage of by all who were permitted to exchange the monotony of a quiet station life for the activity of real useful service, and especially when each man felt that his quota of assistance aided the force whose very existence was threatened by its constant casualties, and which so urgently needed an augmentation of power. The Sepoys well knew the value of officers, and, exposed as they were in the foremost and thickest of the danger, it is not surprising that the loss among them was excessive: one regiment—the Punjab Guide—was thrice cleared of all its officers; and many other corps suffered almost similarly. The Sketch represents the common mail-cart, which was gladly made use of, as being the most expeditious mode of transit; and on this rude and shaky contrivance for hundreds of miles were British officers to be seen incessantly passing on to the scene of action, by day and night hurrying on, only afraid they should be too late to take part in the grand assault which had been expected to come off at any time by a *coup de main*, and which it would have been galling to miss.

When the roads are good, —and this, the Grand Trunk Road, which extends from Calcutta to Peshawur, is, with few exceptions, a first-rate metalled road for a distance of some 1,000 miles,—the carts are drawn by one horse or rather pony, and travel at the average rate of ten miles an hour, including stoppages. Where the roads have not been metalled,—which is done by macadamizing them with a substances called kunkur, obtained in certain localities at a few feet below the surface of the ground, and which, when moistened and then carefully rammed, forms a beautifully hard and level surface,—the carts have a supplementary pony attached. A light awning, supported by two rods and strapped down over transverse strips of bamboo, affords some trifling mitigation from the scorching rays of the sun. But the carts are of the rudest construction, and the springs cannot boast of much elasticity; so that a journey on a mail–cart is reckoned a feat rather worthy of commemoration. The ponies are invariably either vicious or badly broken in, and the delays of starting have to be compensated for by increased velocity in speed : the rate (for the change occurs at every five miles) is generally, when in progress, some twenty miles an hour at the very least.

Capt. G. F. Atkinson, del[t] London, Day & Son, Lithographers to the Queen, Gate Shreet, Lincoln's Inn Fields. E. Walker lith.

No 4. Scene In Camp.

4 A Scene In Camp

THE British soldier who has been accustomed to the small bell-tents of a European encampment is somewhat struck when he first sees the expanse of canvas and the extent of ground occupied in the encampment of a British regiment in India. It is not, however, so much in the tents of the private soldiers (which are not one inch too large for the accommodation of the twelve men for whom they are intended), but it is in the tents of the officers. Commanding officers frequently have a large double – poled tent, measuring thirty feet by sixteen feet; besides one or two other smaller ones, usually single – poled, from fourteen to sixteen feet square; besides an awning and tents for the servants and horses. No fixed rule is adhered to,—every man provides himself as he pleases; and the only necessity that exists, is that the tents must all be pitched with a degree of uniformity, when the nature of the ground will allow of it. The prevailing kind of tent—and Bengal is so celebrated for its tents that it supplies the other two presidencies—is a single-poled tent, about fourteen feet square, with an outer fly or covering, and an outer wall, or *kunaut*, which gives a verandah of from two to three feet in width.

Subalterns, however, are generally content with a smaller kind, commonly called a hill tent, such as is represented in the drawing: it is usually ten feet square, with a double roof but only single walls, and therefore with no verandah; but a strip of canvas extends over the sides a few feet, as a protection from the sun for servants: such a tent can be carried by single camel. The Sketch also shows the manner in which horses are picketed. A rope is fastened to each hind fetlock, and is attached to a peg driven in the ground some few feet to the rear (this prevents the horse from either advancing or going sideways beyond a certain point), whilst to his halter are attached two head-ropes fastened to pegs right and left of him.

The figures in the foreground are enjoying the *otium cum dignitate* in the open air at a time when the sun's rays will admit of such a luxury.

Capt. G. F. Atkinson, del[t] London, Day & Son, Lithographers to the Queen, Gate Shreet, Lincoln's Inn Fields. W. Simpson, lith.

N° 5. Troops Hastening To Umballa.

5 Troops Hastening To Umballa

THE Grand Trunk Road, as has been already stated is the main artery of communication between Calcutta on the east and Peshawur at the north-western extremity of the Indian empire. On this main line, or contiguous to it, are the principal Stations of the Bengal Presidency ; and the amount of traffic is proportionately large. The extent of railway completed up to this time has been of little or no assistance towards facilitating the transport of merchandise, which, up to Allahabad, a distance of 400 miles by land, can likewise be conveyed on the Ganges, either in country boats or on steamers, or on flats towed by steam-tugs. This distance is 800 miles by water, owing to the circuitous course of the river; and although only 400 miles by road, the time occupied in conveying goods averaged from twenty-five to thirty days. Above Allahabad, the only mode of transport was by native carts, which averaged ten miles a day; so that goods that had to be conveyed—say to Delhi, 800 miles from Calcutta—took upwards of ten weeks.

To remedy this dilatory state of things, Dr. Paton, who was postmaster at Allyghur, and to whom also may be attributed the introduction of the mail-cart system, and the accelerated rate of speed, proposed to establish carts between Allahabad and Delhi, to be drawn by bullocks, of which there were to be relays at every ten miles. The scheme was at once adopted, and through its instrumentality goods that occupied ten weeks from Calcutta to Delhi are now conveyed at a uniform average rate of two miles an hour, which reduced the time of transit to seventeen days.

Not only merchandise, but Government stores, and even troops, were forwarded by this "Bullock-train;" and many officers with their families have, after fitting up these carts, made use of them as travelling-carriages, to obviate the more dilatory and expensive process of marching, which involves the purchase of tents and the entertainment of much extra establishment.

The Bullock-train had been extended to Lahore, with a branch running from Umballa to Simla, when the outbreak took place; and, as may be supposed, advantage was at once taken of the opportunity thus afforded of making it useful for the transport of troops to the Camp. The rebels destroyed the carts, and took possession of the cattle, in the neighbourhood of Delhi; but by the assistance of the troops in the service of the Jheend and Puttialah Rajahs, the road was kept free from rebels, and the Bullock-train

reorganized; and throughout the operations before Delhi it proved to be of the utmost importance for the conveyance of troops, who were thus landed at Delhi comparatively fresh. The Sketch represents the style of cart employed, the fore wheels being of the same diameter as the hind ones, and the roof covered with tarred canvas, the sides also being protected by tarpaulins.

Elephants, bazaar ponies, and every kind of vehicle likewise, were immediately put into requisition to expedite the movement of troops.

Capt. G. F. Atkinson, delr London, Day & Son, Lithographers to the Queen, Gate Street, Lincoln's Inn Fields. R. M. Bryson, lith.

No 6. Mutineers Surprised By Her Majesty's 9th Lancers.

6 Mutineers Surprised By Her Majesty's 9TH Lancers

WITH the exception of the European Horse Artillery, of which there were two troops, the 9th Lancers was the only European regiment quartered at Umballa at the outbreak of the Mutiny.

A finer and a better-disciplined regiment was perhaps never seen: it numbered about 700 sabres, and the men, as they afterwards proved themselves to be, were as gallant and distinguished in the field as they were orderly in the cantonment.

This drawing represents a scene which occurred on the march of the force from Umballa to Delhi, and which was subsequently of frequent occurrence.

Large parties of rebel Sepoys were making away with *look* or plunder, and had strings of *hackeries*, or native carts, piled up with treasure, which had been ransacked from the bungalows at Delhi and the adjoining stations. Mess plate, crockery, ladies' dresses, &c. &c., were heaped rudely together, to be sorted and divided at some more fitting opportunity.

The Sepoys one and all were no doubt in great glee at being the happy possessors of so much valuable spoil,-when lo! A small cloud of dust is seen rising in the far-off distance,—and rapidly it approaches,—nearer and nearer it comes, when the tramp of hoofs is heard, and the white dresses of horsemen are seen shining in the sun. There is no time for thought,—no time to yoke the bullocks that still are feeding, and to remove the carts from off the high road, and so escape observation. The Sepoys are numerous,—the approaching force is small ; but they have white faces, and resistance would be of no avail ; but there is no time for discussion,—the advanced guard of the cavalry catch sight of the rebels, and with drawn swords and lances at rest, they apply the spur, and in a twinkling are upon them.

That evening's sun sees that belt of trees with a rebel swinging from every bough. A drum-head court-martial has convicted them one and all. A small native cart is brought under a tree,—the rope is fastened to the rebel's neck and the overhanging branch,—the cart is suddenly driven on, and the miscreant left to swing.

Capt. G. F. Atkinson, del[t] London, Day & Son, Lithographers to the Queen, Gate Shreet, Lincoln's Inn Fields. W. Simpson, lith.

N° 7. Storming The Batteries At Badle – Serai.

7 Storming The Batteries At Badle Serai

It had been a matter of fear in the camp of the small British, force which was on its way from Umballa to recapture Delhi, that the rebels would not fight, and that no opportunity would be afforded of bringing upon them that summary vengeance which they so well merited for their diabolieal acts at Meerut and Delhi. Intelligence, however, reached the camp that the enemy had intrenched themselves a few miles out of the city, and were preparing to dispute the onwards march of our troops. This intelligence proved to be correct, and arrangements were accordingly made for attacking the rebel batteries. At one A.M. of the 8th June, the British troops marched from their encamping, in order to reach the enemy at daybreak. The force was divided into three small brigades ; the first under Brigadier Showers, consisting of H.M.'s 75th regiment and the 1st Fusiliers, who were to deploy to the right of the road ; the second brigade, composed of the 2nd Fusiliers, 60th Rifles, and Sirmoor Battalion, which was to take the left ; and a brigade, consisting of H.M.'s 9th Lancers and some horse artillery, were to make a *détour*, cross the canal by a bridge lower down, and cut off the retreat of the enemy ; while the few heavy guns were to remain in the centre, on the road, and the light batteries to operate on either side.

The troops advanced, and ere the day had dawned, a heavy gun boomed, and a round shot flew down the road, carrying destruction in the British ranks, and giving notice of the proximity of the enemy's position. At once the brigade deployed into line, while the heavy guns replied to the enemy's fire ; but, from superiority of metal and number of guns they had considerable advantage ; having, moreover, the range perfect, and one of the first shots falling among the staff, killing Colonel Chester, the Adjutant-General, and Captain Russell, orderly officer, our artillery was evidently unable to silence the batteries, and fearful was the havoc among the British gunners ; so recourse was had to the cold steel, and the 1st brigade were called up to advance. In the mean time, the General, finding that a heavy fire was directed on the advancing line from the gardens and inclosures to the right, detached the 1st Fusiliers to attack the mutineers, who were there in crowds, and so turn their left flank. Thus H.M.'s 75th foot alone was left to assault the batteries ; and right steadily they advanced, although scarcely a man of it had ever before been under fire, which now was exceedingly heavy, the round shot flying thick into their line, followed by volleys of grape. Thus the regiment steadily advanced, Brigadier Showers conspicuous on a white charger, riding coolly in advance,

as if he was on parade. On he rode, till judging it to be the moment for a more rapid advance, he waved his sword and gave the welcome order, "75th, Charge!" and then with a cheer the regiment sprang forward at the double, amidst a storm of musketry and grape, and the main battery was taken.

The General, in his dispatch, reported that the regiment was gallantly led by its commanding officer,—as, indeed, it was ; but before him rode the gallant Brigadier, whose name was accidentally omitted, and whose distinguished coolness in action, and fearless bearing at all times, made him beloved by the men of his brigade, who, after storming the battery and gaining the heights immediately before Delhi, exhausted as they were, rose and gave him three hearty cheers.

Capt. G. F. Atkinson, del[t] London, Day & Son, Lithographers to the Queen, Gate Shreet, Lincoln's Inn Fields. E. Walker, lith.

N° 8. Outlying Picket.

8 The Outlying Picket

THE Sketch represents a portion of one of the outlying pickets, of which a number were necessarily established in the most advantageous points round the camp. For some weeks little or no protection whatever was afforded to the men, and it was to their own good riles they could trust to having a clear ground in front of them ; but gradually stones were collected, and with a few sand-bags or gabions a rude shelter was obtained. From behind these small light parapets many a rebel was laid prostrate. Many a time, flushed with intoxicating liquors, would large masses threaten to sweep away the picket ; but the steady fire from the British soldier kept them at bay, though at times the assistance of a field-piece was required to drive them back, when the numbers were overwhelming, as they not unfrequently were.

In these pickets the men, harassed by incessant fightings and constant alarms, requiring them to turn out at all hours, were enabled to snatch a brief repose till those on the look-out warned them of an impending attack.

Exposed throughout the heat of the day, and during the wet season, to the heavy drenching rain, it is not to be wondered at that disease did as much execution as the fire of the enemy ; but it was unavoidable, and every man knew it, and bore his share, not without a murmur only, but right gladly and cheerfully, watching with a wistful eye that long red wall, against which he was dying to be led, that he might come hand to hand with that fiendish race who, in cold blood, had butchered defenceless women and hacked to pieces the poor unoffending children.

Capt. G. F. Atkinson, del[t] London, Day & Son, Lithographers to the Queen, Gate Shreet, Lincoln's Inn Fields. E. Walker, lith.

N° 9. Repulse Of A Sortie.

9 Repulse Of A Sortie

During the earlier period of the siege operations before Delhi, the assaults of the mutineers on the advanced post and batteries of the British line were incessant. It is true that the Sepoys very much preferred fighting behind walls and bringing down our exposed troops when they themselves were comparatively secure behind good cover, and it was very difficult to tempt them into the open ; but although this was their prevailing system, there were many exceptions to it.

When the rebels, excited with intoxicating drugs, and compelled by their comrades in the city to go forth and attack the English camp, in order to show that they were true to the rebel cause,—and which ordeal every new comer had to go through before being admitted within the city gates,—on such occasions they were frequently induced to make real assaults. At first the British commanders led their men out of the trenches to attack the mutineers as they advanced ; but as, in addition to being exposed to overwhelming numbers, and suffering heavily on each occasion from the guns on the city walls, the plan was changed and the men kept strictly on the defensive, this to the native mind implied fear ; and the result was what was fully expected, that the rebels would show more pluck and advance right against the batteries, which they frequently did when they had an idea that the men occupying the post were but few in number or exhausted from fatigue. On these occasions, being well primed with *bang*, they would advance against our batteries ; but not a shot would be fired, not a British soldier expose himself, till they began to swarm up the parapet, when, springing up with a volley and mounting the parapets, our gallant men would hurl themselves on to the mass of rebels and mete out summary slaughter, while those who fled were dosed with volleys of grape. The Sketch represents such an occurrence.

Capt. G. F. Atkinson, del[t] London, Day & Son, Lithographers to the Queen, Gate Shreet, Lincoln's Inn Fields. W. Simpson, lith.

N° 10. Reinforcements Proceeding To Delhi.

10 Reinforcements Proceeding To Delhi

The very small force before Delhi, incessantly under fire, was decreasing in numbers so rapidly, while, on the other hand, the force of the enemy was daily and hourly acquiring fresh strength, that it became indispensable that no effort should be spared to push forwards, with the utmost dispatch, every single available soldier. A day—yes, even an hour—was of the greatest importance ; for though each man was ready to yield his life rather than give in an inch, human nature could not long support a continuance of such fearful wear and tear. Exposure to the sun, and with no rest, day or night, except the few snatches of sleep that could be obtained when on duty at the pickets,—continually under a heavy fire, and constantly exposed to hand-to-hand conflicts with the enemy, no flesh could endure such a trial for any length of time ; and the enemy knew this well, and, owing to their numbers, they were enabled to play their own game, and by incessant alarms and threatening of assaults, the poor wearied British soldier was perpetually under arms. The alarm-bugle was for ever sounding, and it was becoming clear to every one that by reinforcements alone could there be any hope of taking Delhi ; for it was as much as the English force could now do to hold their own. It was Sebastopol on a smaller scale, with a battle of Inkermann every other day. Every exertion was therefore made to push down troops ; and among other devices resorted to was the one of carrying the soldiers in panniers slung on camels' backs. In these panniers, or *kujawahs*, the cooking utensils belonging to the companies were usually carried ; but in each of these there was now stowed a soldier ; and by this arrangement he was enabled to proceed some forty miles a day, instead of ten to fifteen, without any further fatigue than resulted from the awkward gait, and consequent uneven motion, of the camel.

The sick were still conveyed in *doolies*, of which one is represented in the foreground. It consists of a simple framework, with a string bottom, on which is laid a thin mattress, while the top and sides are closed in with a red covering of coarse cloth, the whole slung to a stout bamboo, and borne by four natives, of whom there were relays all along the road.

Capt. G. F. Atkinson, del[t] London, Day & Son, Lithographers to the Queen, Gate Shreet, Lincoln's Inn Fields. W. Simpson, lith.

N° 11. Horse Artillery In Action.

11 Horse Artillery In Action

THE Horse Artillery of the Indian Army is on a very different system to that adopted in European armies. In the latter, the guns are drawn by four or six horses, driven, by a gunner for every pair ; while the remainder of the troop are mounted separately ; by which means they are enabled to act as cavalry in defence of their guns. In the Indian Horse Artillery, a gunner is mounted upon every horse. Each system has its advocates ; but unquestionable, so far as efficiency is concerned, nothing can apparently be more perfect than that of the Indian Horse Artillery in the field. In rapidity of movement, rapidity and accuracy in firing, and a wonderful facility of traversing the most broken ground, they are especially conspicuous. During the recent operations, the Commander-in-Chief spoke in the highest terms of admiration of this branch of the service, and repeated what had been so frequently acknowledge before, that the Indian Artillery was second to none, and even, in some respects, surpassed the distinguished artillery of the British army. Not that the officers or men of the Royal Artillery were one whit inferior, or their system imperfect ; but they had been brought up in a different school, and from want of opportunities on actual field service, had not had recently any occasion to take their guns at full gallop over ditches and mud walls, and over the most rugged ground, at a pace that renders it difficult for light cavalry even to keep up with ; while the Indian Horse Artillery, from constant opportunities in the field, have acquired the practice of getting across country in a style that astonished every one who may never before have witnessed it.

The troops that belonged to the Delhi force particularly distinguished themselves, and frequently advanced so close to the walls as to draw the fire of the heavy guns upon them, and to which they replied with their light guns with startling effect. The full dress consists of blue, with gold lace, and a Roman helmet with a strip of leopard-skin round it, and having a crimson horse-hair plume. This was exchanged on service for a light pith helmet, covered with white, and with folds of cloth wound round it, and white jackets and pantaloons, which were gradually exchanged for the all-prevailing mud-colour. Each troop consists of four guns, either 6 or 9-pounders, and two 12-pounder howitzers. Before the outbreak, the Bengal Horse Artillery consisted of nine troops with European, and three troops with native gunners.

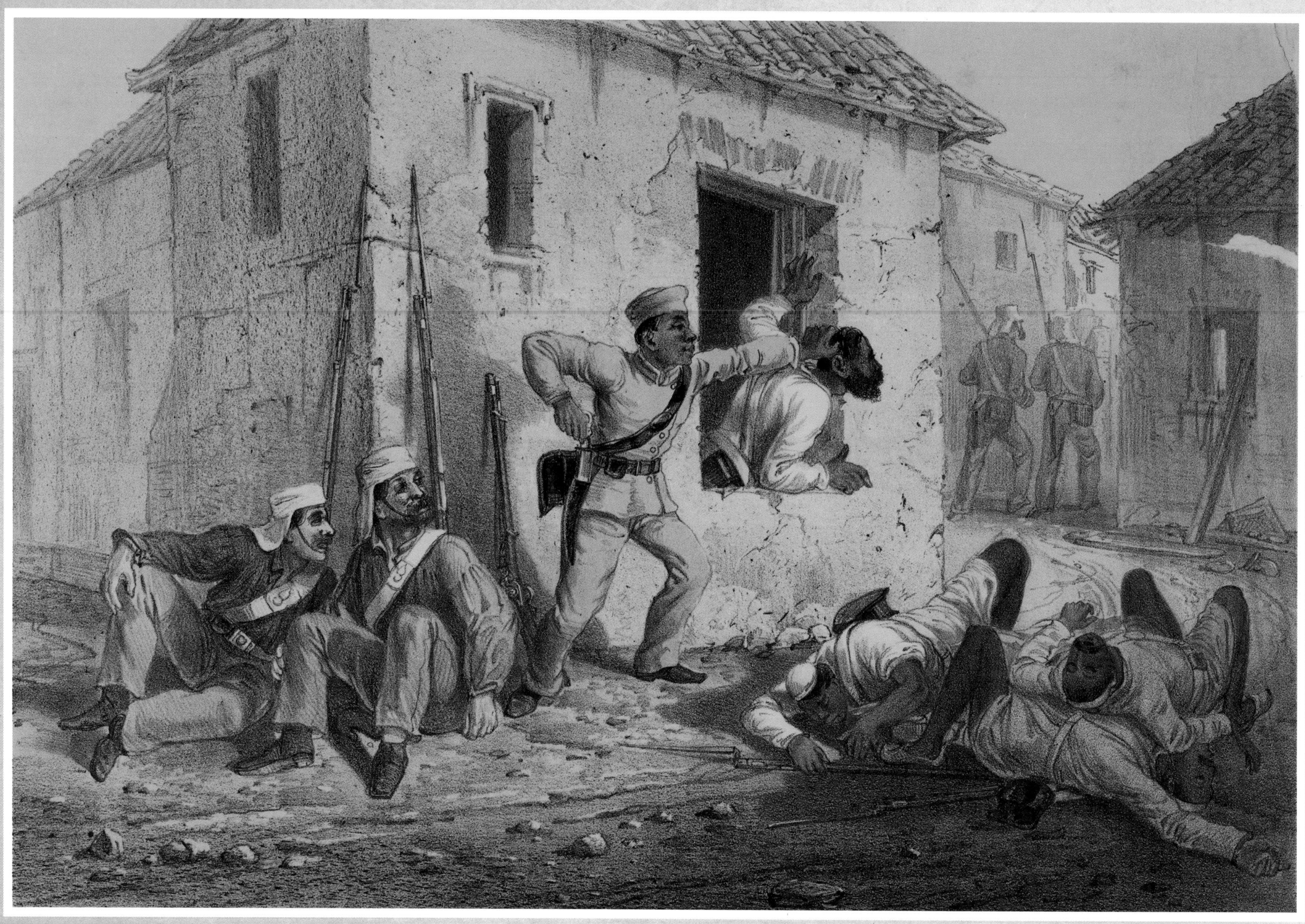

Capt. G. F. Atkinson, del[t] London, Day & Son, Lithographers to the Queen, Gate Shreet, Lincoln's Inn Fields. E. Walker, lith.

N° 12. Incident In The Subzee Mundee.

12 Incident In The Subzee Mundee

As already mentioned, the men of the Sirmoor battalion are chiefly Goorkahs, a race of Hill-men, very small in stature, and with a cast of countenance bordering on that or the Chinese ; high cheek-bones, small eyes, thick lips, and a complexion of a burnt sienna tinge.

These men are of the race that forms the chief force of the army of Nepal, and are descendants of those very men who fought so desperately against us in the Nepalese war : they are a hardy, valiant race of little warriors, cool in action, and with fiery courage in close encounter. During the Sutlej campaign they were a terror to the Sikhs, as, throwing aside their rifles, they drew their short sharp knives, and closed in upon the enemy. The Goorkahs during the whole siege of Delhi occupied the most advanced and the most exposed position on the heights, being quartered at Hindoo Rao's house, which was the key of the British position, and against which the enemy made daily assaults. The losses in the battalion, viz., 319 killed and wounded, out of 450, show how hard must have been their share in the dangers of the siege. More than once it was proposed to relieve them ; but the men, like their gallant commanding officer, Major Reid, begged to be allowed to remain in their dangerous position, which they looked upon as the place of honour.

The Goorkahs have always had a predilection for the British troops, whom they highly respect, but have a signal contempt for the Sepoys, whom they despise, looking upon them as much their inferiors, and reckoning that one Goorkah is at any time a match for three of them.

The men are armed and dressed like the 60th Rifles, whom they had never seen until they met on this occasion, and with whom they at once fraternized in the most friendly manner ; and an honourable rivalry was at once established between them. Posted on the same ridge, ever exposed to the fire of the enemy, men of both corps were constantly to be seen skirmishing and bringing down, at a distance of 1,800 yards, any rebel who dared to expose himself.

The Goorkahs are wonderful shots with their rifles, as indeed are the men of the 60th Rifles, who behaved throughout the operation with the most consummate and conspicuous bravery. The casualties in the latter regiment were 389 killed and wounded, of a force which numbered but 440, until a few days before the storm, when it was reinforced by 200 more.

Besides the rifle, the Goorkah is provided with a knife called a *koorkerie*,—a fearful weapon in his hand, as sharp as a razor ; and wonderfully expert is the owner in handling it.

The Sketch represents an incident that occurred in the suburbs of Delhi called the Subzee Mundee, which is a village situated on the right of the British position, and which was filled with rebels on the first approach of the force, and from which it was most difficult to drive them out, owing to the innumerable inclosure-walls, gardens, and other cover, which prevented the proper advance of our troops. The village was, however, after much fighting, taken possession of, and a strong picket established there ; but up to the very last it was the scene of constant fighting. On one occasion a party of the 2nd Bengal Fusiliers, who were chiefly engaged in that direction, had, with a few Goorkahs, swept down the street and taken possession of the village, when some of the men, with a single Goorkah, sat down to rest, when, from an adjoining window, a Sepoy, who had been concealed in a house, thought to take advantage of the silence to see what was going on. He looked out and stared up the street, when, quick as thought, he was observed by the little Goorkah, who at once sprung up, clutched him firmly by the top-knot on his head, whisked out his koorkerie, and, like a flash of lightning, sliced off his head, and then quietly sat down, as if nothing had happened, to the intense amusement of his British comrades.

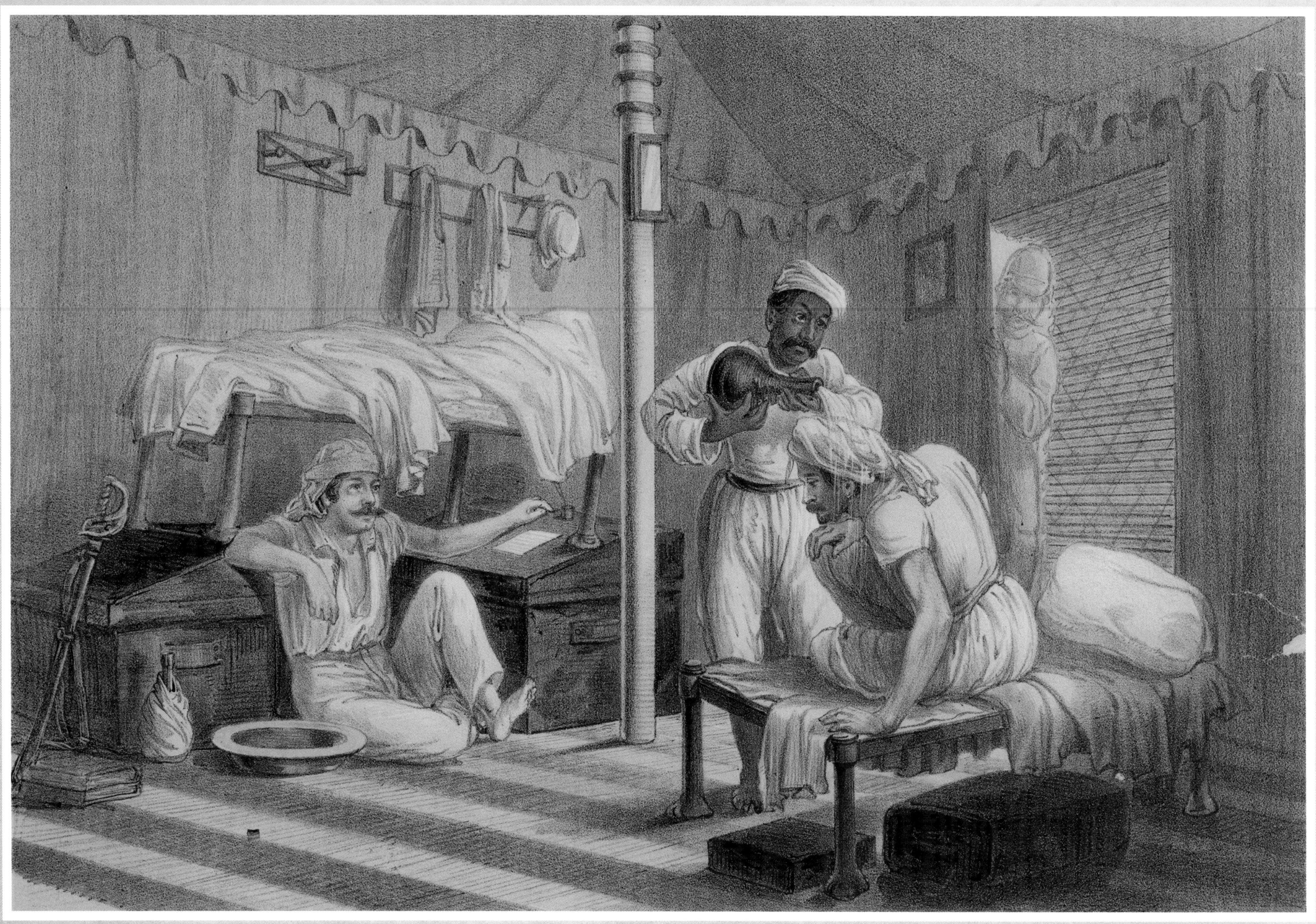

Capt. G. F. Atkinson, del[t] London, Day & Son, Lithographers to the Queen, Gate Shreet, Lincoln's Inn Fields. E. Walker, lith.

N° 13. Interior Of A Tent.

13 Interior Of A Tent

THE exterior view of a hill tent has already been represented. This drawing shows an interior of one which might be thought, in the Delhi camp, to be rather of a superior kind ; for it must be remembered that the movements of the troops were so rapid, and anything like a march at that season of the year had so little entered into the imagination of any one, that no preparations whatever could be made, and those who, at other times, indulged in double or single-poled tents, were now unable, from want of carriage, to take them on ; and so the smallest tents such as are commonly used for dressing in or given up to servants, were gladly made use of, and the bazaars were ransacked of everything that bore even a resemblance to a canvas abode. Thus the officers of the 1st Fusiliers were, from the haste of their departure, unable to take their tents, and they were all huddled together in one large double-poled one, whilst many were only too glad to get hold of a common soldier's tent.

The Sketch them represents one that rejoices in a *setringee*, or floor-cloth, and in *chicks*, or reed curtains, at the doors, to keep out the flies, which, at Delhi, are a perfect plague. The heat is terrific ; the tent is pitched on a sandy piece of ground, and the sun beats right through the thick double roof ; the thermometer stands at 118^{0} of heat. The only resource is to wrap the head in a towel and keep it saturated ; and incessantly has the attendant slave to be summoned to provide a fresh supply of water, as the heat soon makes the towel as dry as chalk. Then, as an additional refuge, the bed is hoisted up on to the camel-trunks, and beneath its thick mattress there is some slight modification of the direct rays of the sun ; but still the heat is prodigious. In vain letters are attempted to be written—the ink has dried up—the pens have split ; and then there goes the alarm—again it sounds—no time to be lost ; the sword is seized from its sheath, which is left behind,—the revolver is laid hold of,—the turbaned helmet is clapped on, and away, right under the burning sun, rushes forth the gallant hero, regardless of heat, or aught that could impede him in his duty.

Capt. G. F. Atkinson, del[t] London, Day & Son, Lithographers to the Queen, Gate Shreet, Lincoln's Inn Fields. E. Walker, lith.

Nº 14. Hodson's Horse At Rhotuck.

14 Hodson's Horse At Rhotuck

Among the many heroes who distinguished themselves during the operations before Delhi, none was more conspicuous than the gallant Hodson, whose glorious achievements had won for him a world-wide reputation. In India his name had long been known as commanding the corps of Guides on the North-west frontier, with which, in countless frays and forays with the wild Hill races, his feats of valour had rendered him and his gallant Guides the terror of the neighbouring disaffected tribes. Removed from his command, and compelled to join his regiment, the 1st Bengal Fusiliers, as a subaltern, he led, what was to him, a life of painful inactivity, until the mutiny broke out, when the Commander-in-Chief appointed him to raise and command a new regiment of horse, to number 2,000 sabres, and which was to bear his name. That name of Hodson was quite sufficient, in the Punjab, to bring to his standard hundreds of gallant Sikhs, who gladly sought to be under his orders. Troops were soon organized at Lahore and elsewhere, and hastened to join the force at Delhi, where Hodson now was acting on the Commander-in-Chief's staff, as also in the Quartermaster-General's department ; not, however, before he had again distinguished himself by conveying despatches to the General at Meerut, across country some eighty miles, through the midst of the rebels. How Hodson was ever foremost in the thickest of every encounter would fill a volume ; mention need only be made here of the affecting meeting that took place between him and his old companions in arms, the gallant Guides, who (a body of horse and foot) had marched from Peshawur to Delhi, a distance of 600 miles, in the unprecedentedly short space of twenty-two days, and joined in a desperate engagement on the very afternoon of their arrival.

With a party of the cavalry portion of the Guides and a squadron of his own Horse, Hodson, with 300 sabres and six officers, sallied forth from camp to intercept a body of rebels who had left Delhi to interrupt our communications with the Punjab. On the first march he surprised and destroyed a party of mutineer irregular cavalry, and then proceeded to Rhotuck, where he found the enemy in no great force, who were soon scattered ; and he and his party took up their quarters for the night in the town. Thinking to make an easy capture of Hodson and his small force, a disaffected Rajah, Babur Khan, collected during the night a horde of rebels, both cavalry and infantry, the greater portion being mutineers from our own irregular cavalry and native regiments, and surrounded the place ; but Hodson,

who had previously sent off his little baggage, and with horses ready saddled, waited his opportunity to sally out. The enemy's cavalry dashed up boldly to the camp, when Hodson's squadrons speedily scattered them, and drove them back.

Then it was that, seeing the numbers of matchlock-men that were brought to bear on his party from gardens and enclosures, he determined to draw them out, and feigned a retreat. The *ruse* was most successful. He had scarcely retired a mile, when the enemy, in full force, with all the pride of anticipated victory, came after him, flourishing their swords in the air and yelling triumphantly, when Hodson, who had now got them into the open plain, gave the words, "Threes about at them!" when he and his men, with a cheer, dashed into the very thickest of them, cutting down fifty in half that number of seconds, and scattering the rest, who fled with dismay.

Capt. G. F. Atkinson, del[t] London, Day & Son, Lithographers to the Queen, Gate Shreet, Lincoln's Inn Fields. J. Needham. lith.

N° 15. Heavy Day In The Batteries.

15 Heavy Day In The Batteries

When the British force first took possession of the heights in the immediate vicinity of Delhi, batteries were at once erected for the few heavy guns that had been brought with the force from Umballa, and those taken from the enemy at the Hindun and at Badle-Serai. These batteries were erected at various points along the ridge, at a range varying from 1,500 to 2,000 yards from the walls. The one in the Sketch represents a portion of one near an old mosque, which was situated about the centre of the ridge, midway between the Flagstaff Battery and Hindoo Rao's. The efforts of the enemy were principally directed against the batteries nearer Hindoo Rao's, which were more accessible ; but the position, even at the Mosque Battery, was far from enviable, as the practice of the enemy was wonderfully accurate, even at that long range, and two of our howitzers were soon dismounted by them. The gunners of the British force were so few, that the duty imposed on them rendered it quite impossible for our guns to cope successfully against those of the rebels, whose artillery was of far heavier calibre, and who had an inexhaustible supply of ammunition, and men in abundance to work the guns. With superiority of fire, coupled with unceasing attacks on the British camp and batteries, to harass and exhaust the few troops that defended them, was the object the rebels had in view ; and this was, perhaps, never more closely on the eve of being successfully accomplished than on the eventful anniversary of Plassey, when the whole strength of the garrison was put forth to overwhelm the British troops, already well-nigh exhausted with incessant fighting and exposure. From daybreak till sunset was one continued conflict under a burning sun : skirmishing and hand-to-hand encounters took place along the whole right of the camp for hours consecutively. But the story can best be told in the words of a distinguished officer, who played a very conspicuous part on that, as, indeed, on every day, from the action of Badle-Serai until a desperate wound, six weeks later, compelled him for a time to cease from taking any share in the operations. He wrote :—"All our troops had now been engaged, and the greater part had fallen back exhausted. The General then directed me to the Mosque Battery, where applications were being constantly sent for reinforcements : I sent every available man. I was then directed to assume command at Hindoo Rao's : when I arrived there, I found every one exhausted and done up ;—there were the 1st Fusiliers and some Rifles, all done up. I went on to the new advanced battery,—it was crowded with worn-out men ; the

artillerymen, likewise done up, had ceased firing ; another party of Rifles, in a similar state, in another position ; 120 men of the 2nd Fusiliers, who had marched twenty-three miles that morning, and had had no breakfast, were lying down exhausted ; three weak companies of Goorkhas were out as skirmishers ; but they, too, were exhausted, and the remainder were resting under a rock. The heat was terrific, and the thermometer must have been at least 140^0, with a hot wind blowing, and a frightful glare. Well, the mutineers all this time, from behind walls and rocks, were keeping up a brisk fire all along our front, *i.e.* to the right of Hindoo Rao's house, as far as Subzee Mundee, and a battery of two guns from Kissengunj was firing upon us without having it returned. I ordered up, when at Hindoo Rao's, 100 of the 1st Fusiliers : after serving out grog to them, I threw them forward to the left front of the new battery. I got a reinforcement of 200 of Rothney's Sikhs, who also had marched twenty-three miles, and had as yet nothing to eat ; and shortly afterwards a small party of 30 of the 2nd Fusiliers, and another under the Sergeant-Major. The latter was sent with the 1st Fusiliers : they beat back the mutineers at once, and took possession of a temple on the left front of the batteries, and which commanded it. On the right I threw forward Rothney's Sikhs, some Guides, and a few of the 2nd Fusiliers : they advanced, and again took possession of Subzee Mundee. Between this and the batteries our skirmishers now had command of the whole ground ; we were now masters of the field,—the mutineers were completely beaten ; and when they found I intended to hold my position, they fell back upon the town. Our loss was considerable,—160 killed and wounded ; but that of the enemy was very severe. We suffered greatly from the sun : the 1st Fusiliers alone had five officers out of ten struck down by *coup de soleil*."

Such is a specimen of the kind of work that the British had to undergo from the 8th of June to the 13th of September ; and small as was the force for the first six weeks,—numbering about 7,000 men of all arms,—the casualities during that time were 22 officers and 296 men killed, and 72 officers and 990 men wounded.

Capt. G. F. Atkinson, del[t] London, Day & Son, Lithographers to the Queen, Gate Shreet, Lincoln's Inn Fields. F. Jones. lith.

N° 16. Fusiliers Bringing The Captured Guns Into Camp.

16 Fusiliers Bringing The Captured Guns Into Camp

THE enemy, having about the latter end of July obtained a vast accession of strength, had assumed a more than ordinary degree of boldness, and their efforts were constantly being directed to force the British advanced pickets on the left,—that is, the stable, mound, cow-house, and other pickets in the neighbourhood of the Metcalfe House. These faced the Cashmere Bastion ; and not content with attacks of infantry, the rebels had caused considerable damage by bringing out field-pieces, which sent round-shot and grape thick among our men. To put a stop to this, Brigadier Showers was directed to make arrangements for getting possession of their guns ; and accordingly, on the morning of the 12th August, he sallied forth with a small force, consisting of 350 men of the 1st Fusiliers and 250 of Coke's Rifles (which two corps bore the chief brunt of the engagement) ; 100 of the 2nd Fusiliers, of the 8th Foot, Goorkahs, and 4th Sikhs ; 100 of H.M.'s 75th, who were on picket at the Metcalfe House, and, accompanied with six guns of horse artillery and a squadron of the 9th Lancers, stole quietly down into the neighbourhood of the enemy, who, in unconscious security, had not withdrawn their guns into the city, but had them all ready for an attack on the British lines that very morning. But the Brigadier was too early for them : ere the day had dawned, the mud-coloured—and therefore difficult to be distinguished—British troops quietly approached, till the rebel sentry calling out, "Hoo kum dar?" (Who comes there?) was replied to by a bayonet thrust through him : but the alarm was given, the rebels sprung to their arms, and a hand-to-hand conflict ensured. Suffice to say that the action lasted about an hour, that an advance was made, and gun after gun captured the rebel artillerymen being bayoneted beside them.

The little expedition was well planned by Brigadier Showers, and was so secretly performed, that those in camp were first apprized of it by the cheering which greeted the victors as they brought into camp, at a gallop, the guns that had just been retaken by them. The scene was as novel as amusing; to behold the horses mounted by infantry, each man carrying his musket with the blood-besmeared bayonets, and urging on the horses at full speed, with a reckless amount of expedition ; the limber and guns encrusted also with infantry, who were enjoying the ride home ; young OWEN, a subaltern of the 1st Fusiliers, who had been wounded on the occasion, occupying a prominent position.

This little action was one of the most successful in the operations before Delhi, and reflected the highest credit on the Brigadier and all who fought under him. Unfortunately the Brigadier was very severely wounded by a bullet in his chest ; but he refused to quit the field, although the General, hearing of it, had sent another officer to relieve him, if he wished. It was not until he had received a second wound, in the hand, and he saw the object of the day gained by the carrying of the guns, that, weak with loss of blood, he gave up the command.

The losses on that morning, considering the sharp nature of the action, were comparatively trifling, being 1 officer and 19 men killed, and 7 officers and 85 men wounded ; but the effects of the action were plain, as the pickets were no longer molested by artillery ; for the rebels felt that to bring them out of the city gates was simply to insure their being captured.

Capt. G. F. Atkinson, del[t] London, Day & Son, Lithographers to the Queen, Gate Shreet, Lincoln's Inn Fields. A. Laby. lith.

N° 17. Sappers At Work In The Batteries.

17 Search For The Wounded

THIS Sketch represents the field of action, when, after an engagement, a search is being made for the killed and wounded. On many occasions before Delhi, it was impossible to remove the wounded as they fell ; often the engagement was carried on in such broken ground, that an advance in any regular formation was impossible, and every man was left to fight his own way along ;—thus numbers fell, and were only missed when the column returned to camp. Then had search to be made, and fortunate was it if a wounded man was found alive ; for, like vultures, the mutineers, from their overwhelming numbers, hovered round as our men retired, and ruthlessly butchered the wounded, and hacked their bodies in pieces. Thus one officer, who was known to have fallen from his horse by a shot through his thigh, but who could not be removed at the time, was sought for in vain that night ; but when day broke, his body was found hacked to pieces.

The Sketch represents a party somewhat more fortunate, as the wounded men have not been attacked by the butchers. The principal figure is a horse-artilleryman, who has found, and is carrying to camp, his poor brother, from whom life has passed away. He is telling, with a throbbing heart, and big tears rolling down his cheeks, to a young ensign, who has questioned him how it happened, the story of his poor brother, and what affliction it will cause his old mother at home, but that he hopes to avenge his loss ; and he is somewhat gratified at recollecting that the last round of grape he had the satisfaction of pouring into the retreating mass of rebels, brought down the author of his calamity.

Capt. G. F. Atkinson, del[t] London, Day & Son, Lithographers to the Queen, Gate Shreet, Lincoln's Inn Fields. A. Laby. lith.

N[o] 18. The Search For The Wounded.

18 Sappers At Work In The Batteries

The Sappers and Miners of the Bengal Army consisted, before the outbreak, of ten companies of Sepoys, who were instructed by their European officers in all the details of that branch of the profession to which they were devoted. When the outbreak took place at Meerut, reinforcements were summoned from every direction ; and among them the Sappers and Miners, who had their head-quarters at Roorkee, on the Ganges Canal, not far from Meerut, were ordered in forthwith. Their commanding officer, the gallant Captain Fraser, had implicit confidence in the fidelity of his men, and felt assured that, though the rest of the army might rebel, his corps would yet remain true to their allegiance. But, poor fellow, his confidence was ill-founded ; for the corps mutinied, and Fraser was shot dead by his own men.

The greater portion, or about 400, who escaped from the sword of the carabinier, made off straight for Delhi, leaving about 150 of their number faithful to their salt. Such an addition of trained men to the rebel force was most invaluable ; for by their aid were they enabled to construct and keep in repair those defensive works which so materially retarded our progress in the capture of the place. As for instance, on one occasion the concentrated fire of our heavy guns was brought to bear on a certain bastion : the fire, so well directed, dismounted the enemy's guns even at a range of 1,600 yards, and demolished the face of the works. An assault was in contemplation ; but, when morning appeared, the bastion appeared stronger than ever ; the injuries had been made good, and a larger number of guns, of still heavier caliber than before, soon sent their shot flying into the British batteries with unerring aim,—so well had the rebels been taught.

And yet it is strange, that, opposed to these were a small remnant of the faithful, who, to the last, worked in the British batteries exposed to the fire of their former comrades, with the greatest intrepidity. The numbers were so few, that a large party of canal-diggers were entertained in the Punjab, and engaged to work, under fire, in the trenches ; and, in addition to these, a large body of common labourers were likewise engaged ; and right gallantly did these novices to the art of war conduct themselves. Directed by a zealous, indefatigable body of young officers, and an able party of non-commissioned officers, who had been recalled from civil duties to devote themselves to their former occupation as Sappers and Miners, the works progressed, assisted by the British troops, who worked hard in the trenches and in the batteries.

And severe work they say it was during the wet season, when the rain fell in sheets, saturating one to the skin, and exposed all the time to the accurate fire of the enemy, whose shells frequently pitched with admirable precision, and burst right in the midst of the working parties, But the works were pushed on, the killed and the wounded were removed, and the *fowrah*, or native spade, was plied more energetically than ever.

Capt. G. F. Atkinson, del[t] London, Day & Son, Lithographers to the Queen, Gate Shreet, Lincoln's Inn Fields. W. Simpson, lith.

N° 19. Advance Of The Siege Train.

19 Advance Of The Siege Train

THIS Sketch represents the advance of the siege-train that was dispatched to Delhi for the purpose of demolishing the fortifications, which, it was found, could not possibly be effected by means of the few heavy guns that originally accompanied the force on its first breaking ground before Delhi.

Anticipating but a trifling resistance, if any, on the part of the rebels, a very few guns were brought from Umballa : these, on the first outbreak of the mutiny, were in the magazine at the Fort of Phillour, under the charge of a Sepoy regiment ; and it was feared that there would be difficulty in obtaining possession of them ; but in consequence of a rapid night march of a wing of H.M.'s 8th Foot from the neighbouring station at Loodianah, the regiment was surprised, and the arsenal secured. An artillery officer was immediately dispatched from Simla by the Commander-in-Chief to bring a third-class siege-train to Umballa, which was accordingly done, by dint of the greatest exertion, and was effected not one moment before it was necessary ; as, immediately after the last gun had crossed the bridge of boats that spanned the then narrow stream of one of the Five Rivers, the water rose, in consequence of the melting of the snows in the Himalayahs, and carried away the bridge. These guns were drawn by bullocks, from eighteen to twenty-four being yoked to each piece.

When it was found that this small train was ineffective to demolish the enemy's works, and that the pieces suffered so much from the accurate practice of the rebel artillery, who dismounted several, even at a range of 1,700 yards, and that the guns were, moreover, injured by the incessant firing, a new siege-train was ordered to be sent from the arsenal of Ferozepore. This magazine being at a distance of nearly 200 miles from Delhi, created considerable delay in the taking of the city ; for nothing could be done but for our troops to maintain themselves in their position until its arrival, which, was not until the 7th of September ; by which time the batteries had been duly prepared for their reception.

The guns of this train were drawn by elephants, as shown in the Drawing,—a single elephant attached to each ; but at times, when the road was deep in sand, the assistance of a second elephant had to be brought into requisition ; and, with a pad to protect his forehead, he would push the wheels, lowering himself on his knees, and showing wonderful sagacity in adopting the best mode of extricating the ponderous mass from its difficulties. The train consisted of nearly fifty pieces of heavy ordnance ; and

these, together with the innumerable carts of ammunition, extended over about seven miles of road, and were protected by British infantry, new Sikh levies, and some irregular cavalry.

Capt. G. F. Atkinson, del[t] London, Day & Son, Lithographers to the Queen, Gate Shreet, Lincoln's Inn Fields. W. Simpson, lith.

N° 20. Troops Of The Native Allies.

20 Troops Of The Native Allies

Amidst the force that was gradually increasing in numerical strength for the grand assault of the city of Delhi, was a motley array of troops belonging to different Rajahs who had faithfully adhered to the British cause ; of whom the most conspicuous throughout the mutiny was the Rajah of Puttialah, whose territory lay in the neighbourhood of Umballa. It was one of the "Protected Sikh States" before the annexation of the Punjab ; and in consequence of the adherence of the Rajah to the British, the state was not confiscated, but additional territory was granted to him as a reward for assistance rendered. When this mutiny broke out, the Rajah at once placed his troops at the disposal of the British Government ; and it is not, perhaps, too much to say, that the safety of Northern India entirely rested on his faithfulness: for it was in his power to have cut off all communication between the Punjab and the Commander-in-Chief's force, which, but for his assistance, could never have reached Delhi ; in fact, the small European force would have had its hands fully occupied in holding its own. The Jheend Rajah and others rendered most salutary assistance ; but the most distinguished character in title was the Maharajah of Cashmere, who at once offered to place a force at our disposal. This offer was at first declined by the rulers of the Punjab, but was subsequently accepted, when it was discovered how essential it was that reinforcements should be supplied, to enable our small force to crush the enemy in his stronghold.

The army of the Cashmere Rajah was composed of different races of men ; principally, however, was it recruited from the hills : it was supposed to be drilled according to European fashion ; but for want of proper knowledge on the subject, the result was anything but advantageous. The moral effect, however, of having the Maharajah on our side, and the mere fact of his having sent a large force to assist in the subjugation of Delhi, was of immense importance, and operated most beneficially towards the object in view ; and lucky for us was it that the moral power was of such advantage, as the positive good that the troops afforded was very questionable. The Sketch represents the troops on the march,—a very irregular body, as may be seen,—scarcely two habited alike, and with arms of every fashion and of every age. The guns were drawn by mules, the cavalry mounted on wretched ponies ; and what with bullock-carts, camels, elephants, sheep, goats, tattoos, women, children, the looker-on would scarcely recognize an army intent upon any really hard work. Efficiency in the field could scarcely be expected ; so that it was

in no way surprising that, when led against the enemy's batteries, the men flinched and fell back, leaving the few British troops who accompanied them to bear the whole brunt of that desperate hand-to-hand conflict that took place at the Kissengunge on the morning of the assault, and which, owing to the flight of the native allies, rendered the attack in that quarter unsuccessful.

Capt. G. F. Atkinson, del[t] London, Day & Son, Lithographers to the Queen, Gate Shreet, Lincoln's Inn Fields. G.M.C Culloch, lith.

N° 21. Storming Of Delhi.

21 The Storming Of Delhi

On the eventful 14th of September, the grand assault of Delhi took place, which, though crowned with success was not effected without a sanguinary struggle, involving casualties to the enormous extent of one-third of the force engaged. Although the British had encamped before the place ninety-seven days previously,—although batteries had been erected, and heavy guns had opened their fire upon the devoted city,—yet this was very soon found to be totally inadequate even to keep down the fire of the enemy, much less to demolish the defences : for ninety days, therefore, it may be fairly considered that the British force merely held its own ground until sufficient reinforcements, coupled with a more efficient siege-train, could be obtained. This was not effected until the ninetieth day, that is, on the 7th of September, when the operations of the siege fairly commenced ; ground was broken that same evening, and on the morning of the 14th the assault was delivered: thus the reduction of the fortified portion of the city was consummated within a period of eight days.

The defences consisted of a massive wall, about 12 feet thick and 16 feet high, supporting a crenelated parapet, with occasional bastions of modern form, which were constructed by our Government some thirty years ago to improve and strengthen the original Mogul fortifications : these bastions carry each from six to fourteen guns. The whole *enceinte* on the land side is protected by a dry ditch, 24 feet wide and 20 feet in depth. The escarp is revêted with a masonry wall eight feet high, above which is a wide berm, from which rises the massive wall already alluded to.

The breaching batteries having been established, and fifty-four pieces of heavy ordnance having opened their destructive fire upon the points selected for assault, the enemy's guns were speedily silenced, and practicable breaches effected. Columns of attack assembled at day break, and were launched against the insurgents' defences, which, by means of escalade, blowing open of the Cashmere gate, and the direct assault of the open breaches, were speedily carried at the point of the bayonet.

But although the main fortifications were thus rapidly taken possession of, the hardest fighting and the most desperate struggles, calling forth the utmost courage and resolution of the gallant besiegers, had now to be encountered. Street-fighting is ever a dangerous and a slaughterous style of warfare, and in this instance was particularly so, as the extent of city that had to be traversed was unusually large ; and, thoroughly defended, as was each nook and corner, from which musketry poured forth destruction into

the ranks of the assailants, it is not surprising that it became the work of many days even for the resolute and daring men who thirsted to annihilate the defenders, who looked not for quarter, to accomplish.

Among the many desperate conflicts, perhaps none was more trying than that which is illustrated in the accompanying Drawing. The 1st brigade, consisting of a portion of the 75th Foot, the 1st Fusiliers, and the 2nd Punjab Rifles, personally led by the gallant Nicolson, had carried the principal bastion by assault, and re-forming behind the Cashmere gate, in the open space in front of the church, were directed to turn to the right, make a circuit of the walls, clearing the rampart as they advanced, with a view to effect a junction with the column that, it was expected, would carry the Lahore gate. The rampart itself was inaccessible ; but below it ran a lane, which in many places was so narrow that four men could scarcely advance abreast ; but, in the midst of a heavy fire, the column dashed on with the utmost intrepidity, clearing the Moree bastion, and inflicting a heavy loss on the enemy, who made a resolute stand at the Caubul gate. Advancing some two hundred yards along the rampart road, formidable obstacles opposed them : a gun, mounted on the rampart itself, and protected by an iron screen, was so depressed as to pour round after round of grape down into the narrow lane, while a gun in advance, protected by a parapet, was likewise fired with deadly effect on the advancing column, while a fusillade of musketry was kept up from the adjoining houses, together with stones and other missiles that were projected upon the devoted heads of the assailants. Again, again, and again did the gallant men advance, and again and again were they mowed down and compelled to desist :—for two hours were repeated attempts made to overcome the defences. Jacob, the gallant commander of the 1st Fusiliers, had already fallen, with many, many others, when the noble Nicolson, who had been with another portion of the column, now joined, and a renewal of the conflict, under his inspiriting example, was begun ; but a fatal ball laid low that gallant hero ; and beside him fell, dangerously wounded, the gallant Greville, of the Fusiliers, and many more. The position of the enemy was too strong, their advantage too great ; and as further attempts involved only the sacrifice of gallant men, the column, as well deserving of imperishable glory as if the attacks had been successful, was withdrawn to the Caubul gate. For ten long hours—for it was now two in the afternoon—had these men been under arms, during the greater portion of which they had been exposed to a murderous fire. Such were the men who fought for the honour of Old England within the streets of Delhi ; and who, day after day for the ensuing week, fought on until the whole city was in their possession ; but for whom it has not been thought worthy to accord a special medal to commemorate this glorious achievement, so truly arduous in its accomplishment, and so beneficial in its results.

Capt. G. F. Atkinson, del[t] London, Day & Son, Lithographers to the Queen, Gate Shreet, Lincoln's Inn Fields. E. Walker, lith.

N° 22. Mutinous Sepoys.

22 Mutinous Sepoys

THIS Sketch represents an interior of one of the batteries, in which are a party of rebel troops. The costume in which these mutineers fought was their usual native dress, upon which were buckled the British accoutrements. This dress consists of a closely-fitting linen jacked, open at the side of the breast, the Mussulman having the opening on the left, the Hindoo on the right. Round their loins a long strip of unbleached cloth, which is wound tightly round and the ends simply tucked in,—this *dhotey* was always worn by the Sepoy beneath his pantaloon, as was the white jacket beneath his regimental coat ; on his head he wore a common white linen skull-cap, and occasionally a turban twisted loosely round his temples, with one end hanging down his back. Frequently, however, the regiments before Delhi turned out in their red coats, with the colours flying and the bands playing ; on one occasion a regiment from the Bareilly brigade marched out, and the well-known music of "Cheer boys, cheer," was wafted by the breeze to the British camp. The Sepoys wear a necklace of white beads, which on the native officers are of gold. In the Sketch, the stout mutineer reposing on his cot is a subadar, or native sergeant-major, as is also the one on the horse, which is caparisoned after the native fashion, and has its mane and legs stained a bright orange-colour.

The Sepoys that composed the Bengal army were a fine body of men ; and it was with a view to secure the tallest and the finest-looking men, that one class—viz., those who came from Oude—were principally selected,—men of high caste, and exceedingly bigoted in their religious views, and which is assigned by many as the main cause of the mutiny having extended so rapidly, as the majority of the army was of one caste, and, it may be said, of one family. The men are tall, the average height being 5 feet 9 inches ; and it was not unfrequent to see grenadier companies with not a man under 6 feet 1 inch. But though tall, and in many cases powerful, muscular men, yet in weight they are not to be compared with the European ; and this may be specially noticed in the tread of a native and of a British regiment. The former pass by with a sort of shuffling pace, while the latter come by with a heavy solid tramp, that seems to shake the earth.

Capt. G. F. Atkinson, del[t]   London, Day & Son, Lithographers to the Queen, Gate Shreet, Lincoln's Inn Fields.   E. Walker, lith.

N° 23. Prize Agents Extracting Treasure.

23 Prize Agents Extracting Treasure

THE grand assault having terminated successfully, and the entire city of Delhi, after a week's hard street-fighting, being in the hands of the British, the more pleasing task of collecting the spoils was now commenced upon ; and no easy work was it for the Prize Agents to secure for the army the spoils they so richly deserved ; for never was more artfully brought into play the cunning and the skill with which the wealthy men had concealed their treasure. Shawls and such-like spoils were more readily obtained, but coin and jewellery, being more easy to hide, the brain had far more effect in discovering the mines of wealth than had the spade ; for it was by judgement—that instigated the piercing into the most improbable places—that at last some key could be obtained to unravelling the mysteries of Oriental concealment. Added to this, the well-known Eastern accomplishment of lying was practised to an unlimited extent ; but the revolver was soon found to be a means of eliciting truth and bags of rupees simultaneously. Treasure was often found in walls duly plastered over, in staircases, between the roof and the beams, and not unfrequently sunk some twenty feet down into the ground, in spots where it was the least expected.

The Sketch represents a scene that occurred. A report had reached the ear of one of the Prize Agents, who of course had offered a large per-centage to those who gave accurate information, that a certain wealthy man had concealed several lakhs of rupees in a certain house. Search was made, but unsuccessfully, the man swearing by everything in creation that he had not a fraction of a rupee concealed. Threats of the rope at last brought out the intelligence that he had some 50,000 rupees in a certain place, but that that was all his wealth. This was speedily extracted, and he was released, when tidings came again that he had not disgorged one quarter of his treasure ; so again was he seized, and, with a revolver at his head, he accounted on the spot for another 50,000, which was as speedily extracted as the former ; but the Prize Agent, convinced that he was still lying, and finding threats unavailing, resolved to establish a little more alarm, placed him as a target, and vowed he would let fly if the fellow did not at once acknowledge where he had concealed the remainder. Still trusting to lies, and little imagining the Prize Agent would keep his word, he again swore most resolutely that he had been disgorged of every pice, and that he really and positively had no more ; upon which the Prize Agent, leveling his revolver, let fly, but purposely avoided

hitting him, allowing the bullet to sing within a few inches of his ear. Seeing that the Agent was in earnest, down went the terrified native on his knees, and declared that he would point out where 100,000 rupees were, if his life only was spared. By such devices large sums were discovered ; but probably one-twentieth of the actual wealth of Delhi was never obtained to reward the captors for the many weeks of privation, danger, and death that they were exposed to ere the city fell into their possession.

Capt. G. F. Atkinson, del[t] London, Day & Son, Lithographers to the Queen, Gate Shreet, Lincoln's Inn Fields. W. Simpson, lith.

24. Capture & Death Of The Shahzadaghs.

24 Capture And Death Of The Shahzadahs

One of the many acts that distinguished the career of the gallant Hodson has already been illustrated in these pages ; the next most important feat which made his name so prominently conspicuous, was his capture of the King of Delhi. From information obtained through spies, it was ascertained that the King had taken refuge at Humayon's tomb, about seven miles from Delhi, with a large armed force : Hodson, with fifty troopers of his regiment, sallied forth, resolved, at all hazards, to endeavour to secure him ; armed, however, with instructions that he was to promise the King life and freedom from personal indignity. With his small escort he rode up to the neighbourhood of the tomb, and concealing himself and his men in some old building, sent in his emissaries to Zeenat Mahal, the King's favourite wife, with the ultimatum. After two hours of suspense, the emissaries came forth to say the King would deliver himself to Captain Hodson only. Right into the thick of the King's force then rode Hodson boldly, with his small escort, when the King came out of the gateway in his palankeen, and asked if it was "Hodson Bahadoor," and if his life would be spared ; upon which Hodson renewed the promises already made, but threatened to shoot the King on the spot if an attempt at a rescue were made. The King then gave up his arms, which Hodson handed to his orderly, still keeping his own sword drawn ; and so brought the venerable puppet a prisoner into the city.

This was not sufficient to satisfy Hodson, who was bent upon capturing the two sons and the grandson of the King, viz. Mirza Moghul, Mirza Kheyr Sultan, and Mirza Aboo Bukker, who had taken such a prominent part in the atrocities of the 11th of May. This was an act that required no ordinary amount of daring ; for although the King himself had authority sufficient to check the turbulence of the fanatics who surrounded him, it was a different thing in the case of the sons, who, it was supposed, would offer resistance. But Hodson had the courage to face it, and with 100 picked men of his regiment, and accompanied by his second in command, M'Dowell, of the 2nd Fusiliers, he rode again, on the following morning, to within a short distance of the tomb, and sent in emissaries to say the sons must surrender, and surrender unconditionally, which, after a very considerable delay, they accordingly did, feeling confident that, sooner or later, they must be taken, and imagining that, like the King, their lives would be spared. But this was the moment that called for coolness and judgement on the part of Hodson, as, though the sons delivered themselves up, the crowd of fanatics, numbering some 6,000, seemed disposed

to prevent it, and a collision was impending, when, by a dexterous movement of his troop, the cart, drawn by bullocks, upon which the sons were seated, was separated from the crowd, which gradually and sullenly fell back towards Humayon's tomb.

Ten troopers were sent on with the cart, and, with the rest of his men, Hodson rode after the mob, and, leaving his party at the gateway, with M'Dowell and four men, rode right up the steps into the archway where the rebels had assembled, and ordered them to lay down their arms. "There was a murmur,—he reiterated his command, and (God knows why), I never can understand it," wrote the gallant but unfortunate M'Dowell, "they commenced doing so." There the party remained for two hours collecting the arms, and in full belief that they would be rushed upon ; but a cool, bold front deterred the rebels from the attempt. Carts were then procured, and loaded with the weapons ; when Hodson and his troop quietly withdrew, the crowd following them closely. Then, galloping after the King's sons, Hodson caught them up just in time ; for the crowd, which had followed them, had increased in numbers, and their gestures and movements indicated an attempt at rescue. Not a moment was to be lost,—Hodson and his small party were but as a log in the ocean ; so, addressing rapidly a few words to his men, he himself removed all the object of a rescue, by at once shooting the three blood-thirsty scoundrels, whose bodies, flung on to the cart, were then conveyed into the city, and exposed in the most public place, on the very spot where they had themselves, three months previously, directed and witnessed the butchery of unoffending women and children.

Capt. G. F. Atkinson, del[t] London, Day & Son, Lithographers to the Queen, Gate Shreet, Lincoln's Inn Fields. T. Picken, lith.

N° 25. Wounded Officers At Simla.

25 Wounded Officers At Simla

SIMLA is a sanatarium in the Himalayahs, and is situated on a range of mountains about 7,500 feet above the level of the sea ; but there are many houses perched upon a loftier range, at a level of 8,000 feet. It is at a distance of forty miles from the plains, the old road from which first ascends to Kussowlie, and attains the 7,500 feet in a length of nine miles : it then descends again to Subathoo, and by continual ascents and descents at last reaches Simla, which has become the most fashionable of all the summer residences in the Himalayahs. The houses are principally built in the neighbourhood of the bazar, contiguous to which are the church, reading-rooms, assembly-rooms, theatre, &c. ; but for two miles in either direction, on every accessible spot where a structure could be build, have small rustic dwelling been perched.

The roads are all railed in ; and throughout the length of Simla, which extends over four miles, is tolerably level, and upon which, as the pedestrian has good reason to confess, ladies can gallop their horses at full speed. Here the Governor-General resided for several hot seasons, as did also the Commander-in-Chief ; and here flock hundreds of officers, with their families, who can be spared from their regiments during those months of the year when military exercises are suspended. Here were assembled scores of officers who had been sent to a bracing and invigorating climate to recover from their wounds, or from the sickness which had fallen on them before Delhi.

The common style of conveyance in the hills is a *jampaun*, which is represented in the Drawing ; consisting of a sort of sedan-chair, but carried by four men. It is provided with a shifting top, which consists of four upright rods, supporting a painted canvas roof, and having curtains of black blanketing which is impervious to the wet.

The roads being level, and well railed in, any kind of horse can be ridden at this hill station ; but ponies are most preferred ; of which excellent one, born and bred in the inner hills, are greatly prized, as being very sure-footed, and accustomed to traversing, securely, steep and broken roads.

The air of Simla was wonderfully efficacious in restoring the wounded to health : men who were brought up almost lifeless, were to be seen visibly improving day by day ; and the weak and emaciated rapidly recovered their strength, and were soon, in many cases, so far restored as to justify their returning to Delhi to take part in the final assault.

Capt. G. F. Atkinson, del[t] London, Day & Son, Lithographers to the Queen, Gate Shreet, Lincoln's Inn Fields. T. Picken, lith.

N° 26. Wounded Men At Dugshai.

26 Wounded Men At Dugshai

THE position and characteristics of the station of Dugshai have already been detailed. Situated at a very lofty elevation, it was singularly well adapted for the reception of the sick and wounded soldiers, as the barracks, in consequence of the departure of the 1st Fusiliers, who had occupied them, were now available.

Kussowlie was nearer the plains, but the barracks there had been given up for the use of the wives and families of officers, who, for greater security, had been ordered away from Umballa, that they might enjoy the protection of the small European force, chiefly convalescents, who remained there. Some slight defences had been erected, and the verandahs of the barracks were barricaded , and supplies laid in : so was it at Dugshai. A panic had fallen upon the resident at Simla, in consequence of some misapprehensions, arising from certain unfavourable acts of the Goorkah battalion quartered in the vicinity ; upon which a flight was made direct for Dugshai, that safety might be secured behind English bayonets. Ladies, to whom the thought of walking even one mile would have been appalling, now, inspired by fear, actually walked (and in some instances carrying children) the whole distance of nearly forty miles ; for the flight was precipitate, and neither conveyances nor horses could be procured. In the Dugshai barracks they sought refuge, and, in full anticipation of the place being assaulted, barricades were erected, and other defences instituted ; but the alarm passed away, and the cholera broke out, and the refugees fled back more precipitately then they came. Here men of the Fusiliers, Artillery, Lancers, and other regiments, were to be seen enjoying the truly exhilarating air, after the terrific heat and exposure to which they had been subjected. Wounded men—some desperately, others dangerously, but still able to crawl out—were to be seen sitting together on benches, or lolling on the greenswards, fighting again their battles, and now laughing merrily over scenes which were anything but amusing at the time of their occurrence.

The barracks at Dugshai are covered with shingle,—that is, with strips of wood, laid on slate fashion, which, according to the back-wood American system, is the prevailing kind of roofing in the Hills, where timber is plentiful : the walls are of rubble masonry.